THE WISH BOOKLET

Fashion 1861 - 1865

By Susan Bonsall Sirkis

Copyright 1965, by Susan B Sirkis

All rights reserved. No part of this booklet may be reproduced without permission of the author.

ISBN 0-913786-01-2

5th Reprinting

Miss China, Miss Wax, and Miss Rag, made and dressed according to directions and instructions in the WISH BOOKLET.

THE WISH BOOKLET

This is called the WISH BOOKLET because I wish it could be longer and because I wish that you will feel that way too. I have never read or studied a good costume book without wishing that it were several hundred pages longer.

Most frequently I receive the queries, "How shall I dress my Scarlett O'Hara?" "How shall I dress my Little Women?" "How shall I dress my Civil War China?" Here then is the answer. If you make all of these clothes for one doll - my, what a wardrobe she will have. And if you dress ten dolls from these patterns they will all be very well dressed. By following the patterns and suggestions in this book you can make innumerable outfits - all different. This book is a detailed survey of the fashions over a four year period - the years of the American Civil War. They are American fashions but they have as a background the two countries which contributed most to fashion during the period, France and England. Thus you may use them for any character doll of the period.

The Middle Victorian era is one that we all like, for who does not respond to the romance of the hoop skirt and the languorous ladies of the period? And which of us does not thrill to the sight of dozens of small garments that present the flavor of our favorite time.

The wax doll in the picture was made by a good friend of mine, Carolyn Milholland, who also supplied the body pattern, and the incentive needed to get this booklet completed.

As you will notice, there are no instructions given for enlarging the patterns to fit other sizes. However the patterns are fairly simple and once you have made them in the size given, you will probably be able to make them in any size.

I cannot stress too much the importance of smallness in the making of these garments. Everything should be in proportion. Your thread should be light, your needle thin. Your stitches should be infinitesimal. A stitch that is too long will contribute just as much that is undesirable to the garment as a ribbon that is too wide or a material that is too thick.

There are of course people to whom I must say thank you; Mrs. Fisher, who has been my friend for several years now and as the years increase I value the friendship and the encouragement more; Fawn Zeller and Lucile Clay who are constant reminders of what talent, ingenuity, and needle and thread can accomplish; and of course, my family, who all understand that things like this take time.

Good luck to all of you - may this booklet provide you with something to dream over, something to wish for, and finally, something to do.

West Point, New York
October 1965

Susan B Sirkis

BODY FOR CHINA DOLLS

Make the body of muslin. Sew center front seam and center back seam on torso. Sew curved side of seat to bottom of back. Sew seams in leg. With leg inside out insert leg. You will have to adjust the leg length according to the length of the china foot. The length of the combined leg should equal the torso and head together. Wrap thin wire tightly around groove in china leg. Make sure that the seam is in the back. Turn leg. Stuff with cotton or sawdust to x. Insert needle at back, come through to front, take a small stitch bringing needle out back. At the same level pick up first one side, and then another and draw towards the center back of the leg. This makes the knee joint. Continue stuffing to solid line. Baste tops closed. Turn body inside out. Baste tops of legs to free edge of seat section. The legs should be inside the body. Then sew bottom of seat to bottom of front. Turn body and stuff firmly to solid line. Make an envelope fold at top. Sew closed. Cut a piece of fabric wide enough to go around top of arm and long enough so that doll's hand hangs a little below hip line, with a little to spare. Seam long edges and join to arm by the same method used for the leg. Do not stuff upper arm. Sew arms over top of body. Loop pieces of narrow cotton tape through sew holes in doll's bust. These should extend to waist. Whip head to body.

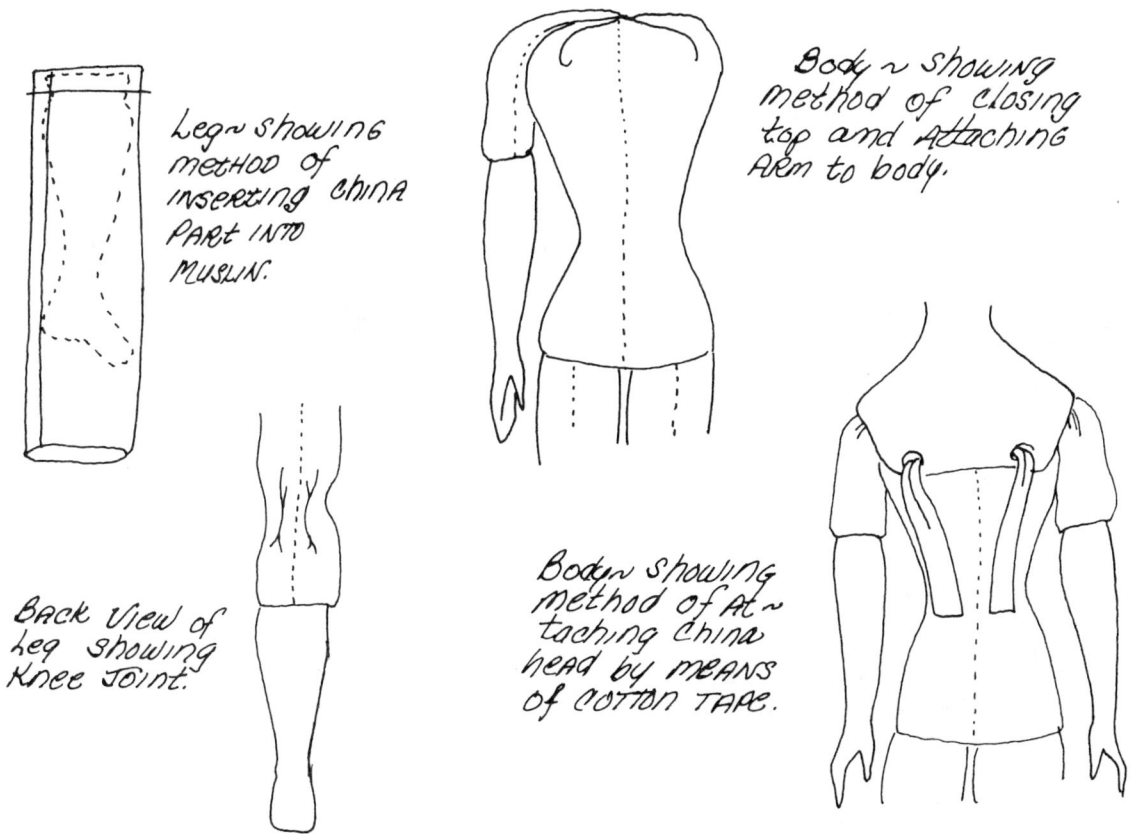

Leg ~ showing method of inserting china part into muslin.

Back view of leg showing knee joint.

Body ~ showing method of closing top and attaching arm to body.

Body showing method of attaching china head by means of cotton tape.

PATTERN FOR A RAG DOLL

Make the doll of any appropriately colored cotton or muslin. Before any sewing is done trace the face onto the front section. Fill it in, either with embroidery floss, using one strand, or textile paints. You may also use oil paints, of course. Sew darts in the front and backs. Sew center back seam. Sew curved side of seat to bottom of back. Sew back and front together, gathering front at double dotted lines so it fits the back. Leave bottom and top open. Sew the leg seams. Turn inside out. Whip the bottom of the foot to bottom of the leg. Turn and stuff. Stuff to x. Make the knee joint according to instructions given in pattern for the china doll. Sew to right side of torso front. Stuff torso to neck. Whip seat to back of legs. Stuff neck and head. Gather top of head and whip closed. Sew arms together. Back stitch on dotted lines to indicate fingers. Stuff. Sew to shoulder.

You may make the hair of light weight yarn, embroidery floss, mohair, or, of course, real hair. Some suggestions for its arrangement are shown in the sketches.

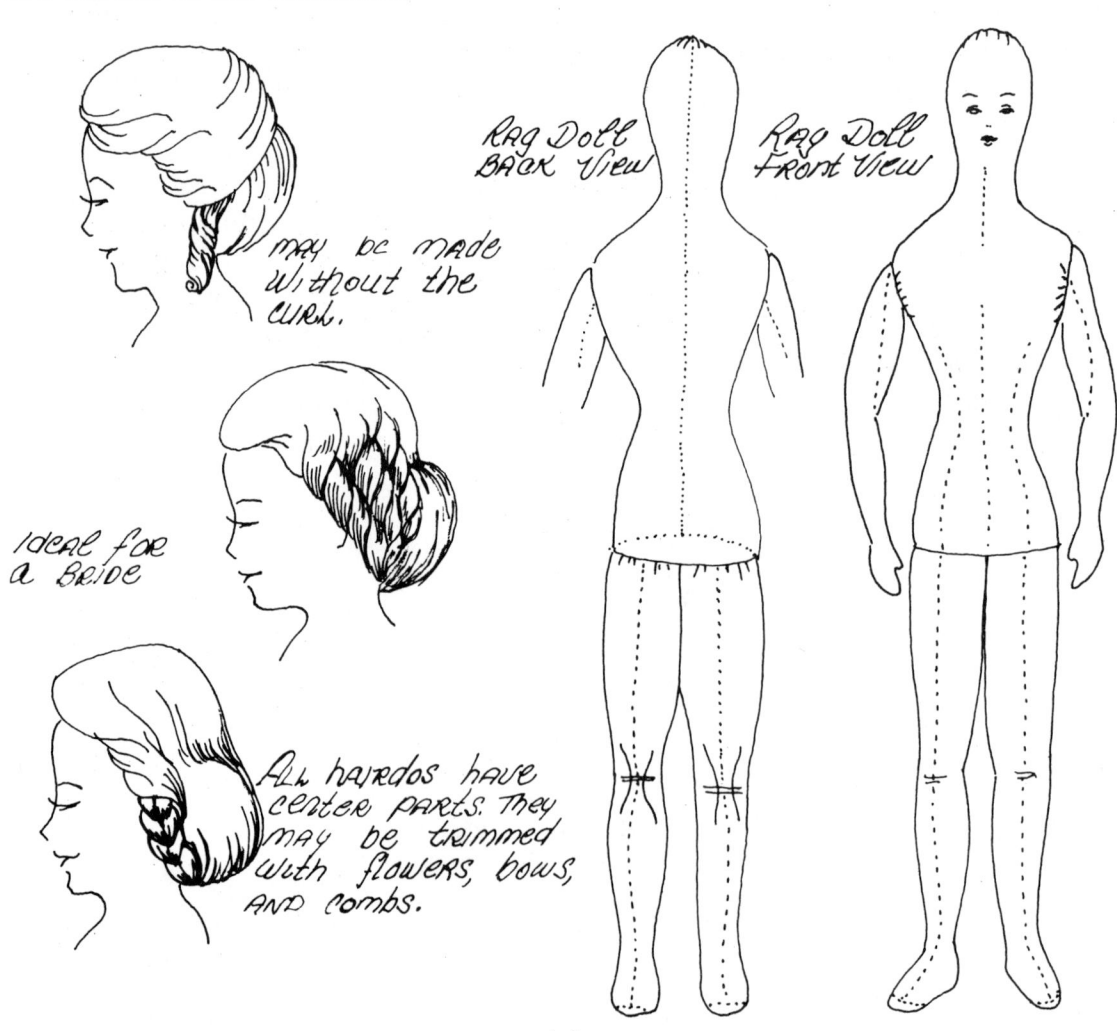

May be made without the curl.

Ideal for a Bride

All hairdos have center parts. They may be trimmed with flowers, bows, and combs.

Rag Doll Back View

Rag Doll Front View

LINGERIE

These little items of doll underwear are to me the most fascinating part of doll dressmaking. All the dainty laces and soft material and all the tucks and ruffles - they take time but they add so much charm. I always use batiste for the underwear, with the exception of the corset. I embroider the doll's name on all the garments, always close to the hem in front. I also color co-ordinate, using ribbons and bows, and embroidery floss all of the same color, so that the doll has a set of matched underwear. All seams should be French seamed together.

#1 - CHEMISE Cut a piece of fabric ten inches by six inches. Seam together two short ends, leaving one and one fourth inches open for placket. Hem placket. Make a one half inch hem in the bottom. Lay the garment down so the seam is at center back. Cut one and three quarter inch slashes down each side. These will be the armholes. Whip a quarter inch lace edging to these. Tack corners together. At center front whip down a narrow strip of fabric one and one quarter of an inch long which you have trimmed with narrow lace. Run a gathering thread around neck. Put on doll and draw up to fit around shoulders. Bind top with narrow binding made of self-material. Close with button and loop. Trim front with two small buttons and a bow.

#2 - OPEN PANTALETS Make hems in bottom. Make pintucks on solid lines. Trim bottoms with ruffles of half inch lace. Sew seam BC on each leg. Hem edges AB on each leg. Run a gathering thread through tops and draw up to fit waist. Sew to a waistband, closing at center back with button and loop.

#3 - CORSET Make the corset of strong fabric that does not fray easily, such as sailcloth. Sew seam CD, center back, and seams AB, sides. Whip a piece the size and shape indicated by shaded area to each front. Leave the top edge open. Sew one fourth inch cotton tape to dotted lines and over all seams. This is the casing for the stays. Use pipe cleaners for stays, and stuff pockets at top with cotton. Narrowly bind all edges with silk seam binding. Work eyelets on both sides of front. Trim top with ruffle of one half inch lace. Lace front with narrow silk ribbon.

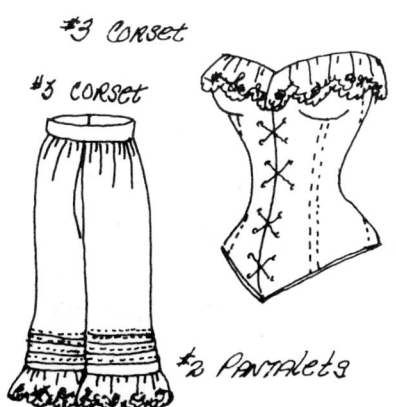

#4 - UNDER PETTICOAT   Cut a piece of fabric twenty-one inches by six and a half inches. Seam the short ends together. Using bottom of pantalets as a guide make four pintucks in the bottom and hem. Trim bottom with a ruffle of three fourths inch lace. Make a casing in top. Run narrow tape or ribbon through casing and draw up to fit doll.

#5 - STOCKINGS   Using #1 steel knitting needles and #30 white crochet cotton, cast on fourteen stitches. Work in Rib stitch (knit one, purl one) for one half inch. Work in stockinette stitch (knit one row, purl one row) for four inches. Using white sewing cotton, run a thread through all loops on knitting needle. Draw up all stitches and secure. Whip back edges together.

#6 - HOOPS   Cut two pieces of wire sixteen inches long. Cut eight pieces of tape five inches long and eight pieces of tape one and a half inches long. Join the two wires into circles. (Use a light wrapping of adhesive tape to join ends.) Wrap both circles with tape or ribbon. At equal distances around one hoop sew one end of each of the five inch tapes. Join the other ends to a waistband. Sew one end of all of the shorter tapes to the same hoop between the longer ones. Sew the free ends of these to the other hoop. Close waist with a hook and eye.

#7 - PETTICOAT   Cut a piece of fabric twenty-five inches by six and a half inches. Seam the short ends together, leaving one and a half inches open at the top for placket. Hem placket. Make a one half inch hem in bottom. Trim bottom with three one inch lace ruffles and small bows. Gather top to fit waist. Attach to a waistband and close with small button and loop.

#8 - NIGHT GOWN   Sew shoulder seams. Cut a strip of fabric a quarter of an inch wide and about twenty-three inches long. Make a narrow binding by pressing under folds on each side. Whip narrow lace to either side of a seven and a half inch strip of the binding. Fold fronts

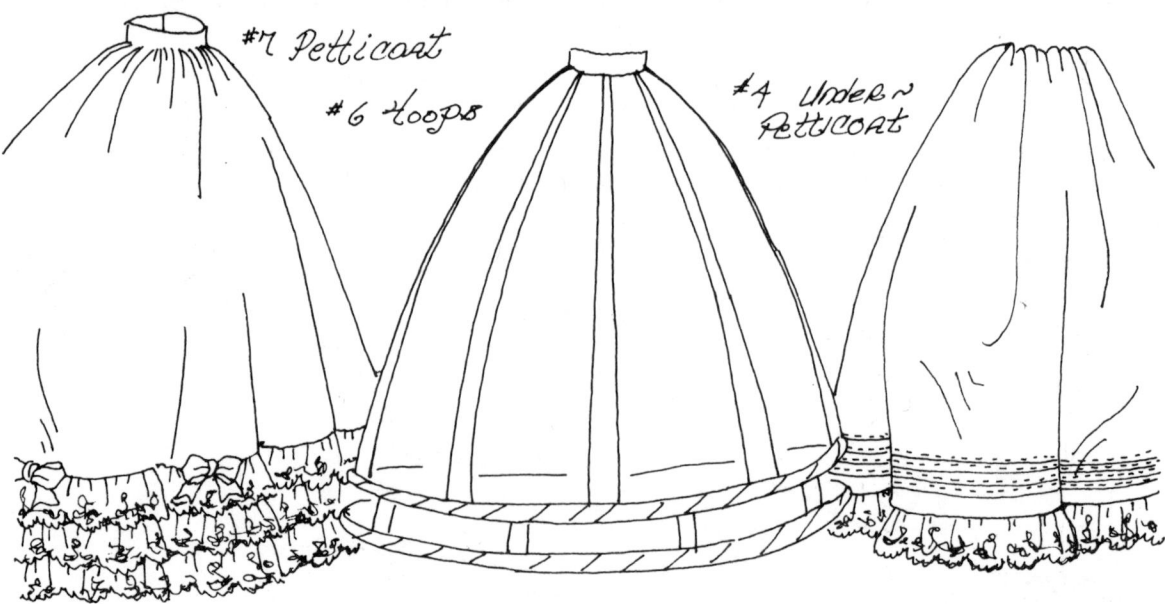

under and hem. Sew trim down right front with stitches concealed in hem. Cut remainder of binding to equal in length the solid lines around shoulders. Trim these three strips all around with narrow lace and baste in place. Make French knots with two strands of embroidery floss about one eighth inch apart down center of binding strips. Sew tiny buttons to dots on left side of front and work buttonholes on right. Make a lace collar and whip in place around neck. Gather top of sleeve to fit armscye. Gather bottoms to fit over hands. Bind narrowly. Trim with lace ruffle. Hem bottom of garment.

    #9 - WRAPPER Make wrapper of pastel flannal, lined with silk. Sew shoulder seams. Gather tops of sleeves to fit armscye. Sew underarm seams. Trim all edges with narrow lace, or other narrow trim. Sew hook and eye to waist line. Tie a velvet ribbon around waistline.

    #10 - NIGHT CAP Gather on dotted lines. Draw up to fit seam A. Sew together. Gather bottom of back to fit back of head. Trim all around with ruffle of narrow lace. Trim center back with bow of narrow ribbon. Sew narrow ribbon to X's for chin ties.

    #11 - SKIRT SUSPENDERS Cut a piece of narrow tape long enough to go around waist. Sew two four inch lengths to the front about three quarters of an inch apart. Close tape around waist with a hook and eye. Pin little safety pins to dangling ends. By pinning these to the front of the skirt about two inches above the hem, the skirt will be raised to display the underskirt.

SHOES

#12 - BOOTS Cut two soles of cardboard and two of black leather. Cut the heels either of wood or cardboard. Paint them black. Cut two toes of soft black leather. Cut the uppers of soft leather, in a light color. Glue the toes firmly to the uppers, butting the edges of the uppers together to form the seam. Turn shoe inside out and sew the back seam. Turn. Glue upper to cardboard. Glue the leather sole over the cardboard, sandwiching the seam allowance of the upper between the two soles. Glue the heel in place. Punch holes in upper with sharp needle, or use tiny eyelets. Lace with heavy black thread.

#13 - EMBROIDERED SLIPPERS Draw the design on a piece of satin. Embroider with single strand of embroidery floss. Cut the pattern out of tissue paper. Centering the design over the paper glue the tissue to the back of the embroidery. Trim the satin leaving about one eighth of an inch all around. Sew or glue back seam. Cut two soles for each foot, one of brown paper (grocery store type) and one of black leather. Fold material of upper over brown sole, glue in place. Then glue the leather sole in place. Glue the excess material around top of upper under. With a little extra patience you can line the slipper. This has to be done before you sew the back seam.

#14 - DRESS SHOE Make this of soft leather or fabric to match the dress with which the shoes are to be worn. Use the pattern for the slipper with the addition of the heel of the boot. Trim the instep with little buckles, bows or flowers.

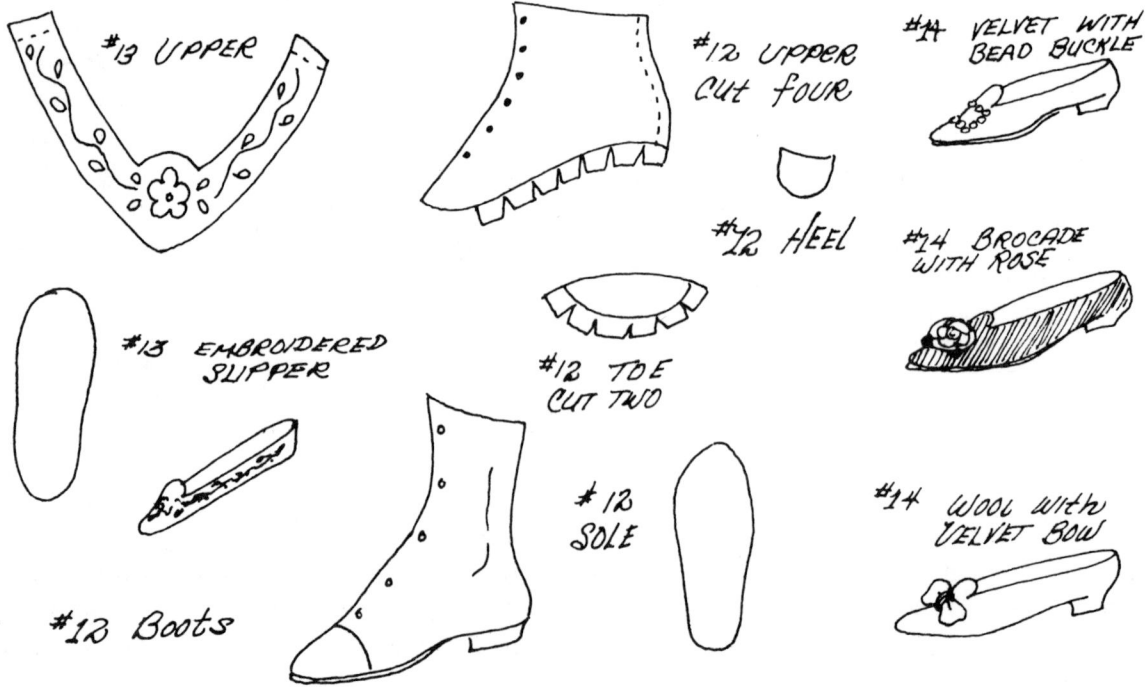

- 8 -

#15 - SKIRT

Before you commence with the business and pleasure of making the dresses it will be necessary for you to make a skirt pattern. The size of this booklet prohibits my giving it full size. Take a piece of tissue paper seventeen inches by sixteen inches. Following skirt diagram A draw your pattern according to dimensions given. Following skirt diagram B mark your skirt pattern with the sewing particulars. Always leave skirt open from waist to dot for placket. Always adjust hem after skirt is trimmed and sewn to waistband. Some of the bodices are finished separately from the skirt. In this case the skirt should be bound narrowly as possible. If you are using a fairly heavy material for the skirt use batiste for the waistband, to reduce bulk. Close backs with hooks and eyes. Small hooks should be sewn to the bodice side seams and the hooks to the corresponding place on the skirt to hold them together. When necessary the placement of the skirt trim is given on small skirt diagrams in the pattern section. These should be drawn onto your tissue pattern and followed in the usual manner. The skirts are not to be lined.

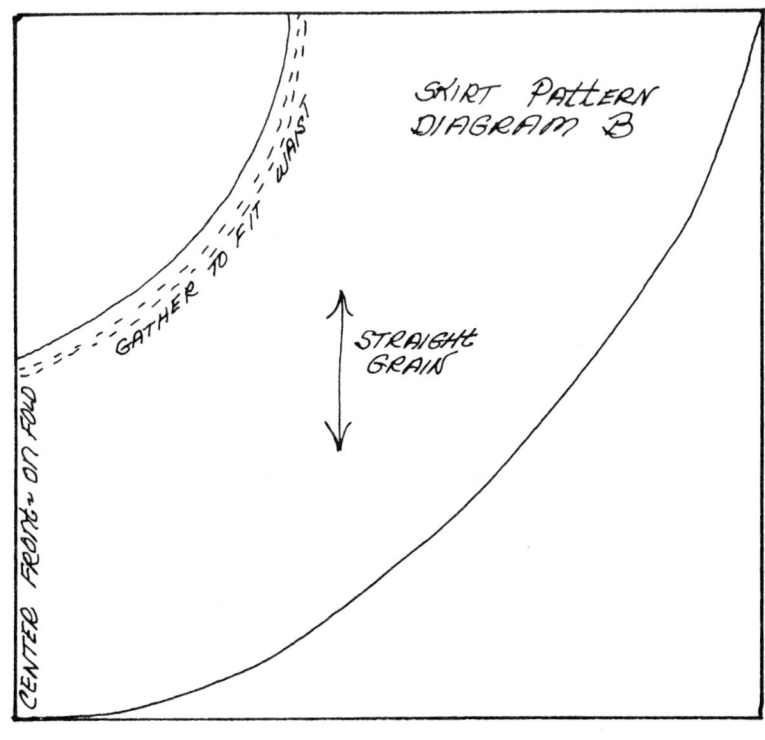

#16-MORNING DRESS Make the skirt of brown poplin. Trim it around the bottom with two rows of black lace. Scatter jet beads over the pattern of the lace. Put a ruffle of self-material around the bottom. Make the bodice also of brown poplin. Join back side pieces to center back, matching double notches. Make the darts in fronts. Join shoulder seams. Sew sleeves to armscye. Join underarm seams. Bind the bottom of the bodice and sleeves with narrow self bias binding. Trim with a band of black lace and jet. Place band of similar trim over seam joining sleeve to bodice. Tack a narrow lace ruffle to inside of sleeve edges. Make black buttons and loops. Trim collar with a narrow ribbon bow.

There was great inventiveness used by the women of the early sixties in the design of their clothing. They had dresses for the home, for visiting, for tea time, for dinner. It is hard for the American woman of today, who casually changes from the shorts in which she has spent her day to the cocktail dress in which she will spend her evening (both items of clothing unknown to her Victorian ancestress) to imagine a way of life which prompted so much daily changing of clothes. When a woman rose in the morning she laced herself into her corset. She put on a simple morning gown in which she ate her substantial breakfast. If she planned some sort of outside activities after breakfast she changed into suitable garments designed for the purpose.

For luncheon she put on a home gown suitable for receiving any guests who might be present. After this strenuous morning who can blame her for retiring to her room and loosening her stays for a few minutes before donning her visiting dress and going naturally enough, visiting? When she returned from her visits it was time to change for dinner, and after dinner she had to change into suitable attire for the evening's entertainment. Even the woman who ran her own home? She changed from a house dress and apron to a clean house dress and apron before dinner. It is hoped that she also found time to loosen her stays.

#17 - ROBE DRESS   Make the skirt of white organdy. Do not mount on waistband. Trim by whipping black moire ribbon three fourths of an inch wide to shaded areas. Use ribbon one fourth of an inch wide for band around bottom of skirt. In circled areas trace bird and flower design lightly in pencil. Color with textile paints or embroider with two strands of embroidery floss. Or use segments of black lace, appliqued, to build up design. Make the bodice of white organdy. Use nightgown (#8) sleeve pattern. Shaded area is black moire whipped down. Small black buttons should be sewn down front. **Sew back side pieces to backs. Hem backs.** Close back with three small buttons and small buttonholes. Sew shoulder seams. Set sleeves into **armscye**. Gather bottom of sleeve to fit over hand. Bind bottom with black moire. Sew underarm seams. Gather top of skirt to fit top of bodice. Sew together. Place a small hook and eye at waistline, center back. Make a narrow belt of black with a flat bow at center front and a hook and eye at center back.

You may substitute a colored ribbon for the black, if you prefer. This dress is designed to represent one of the many designs for fabrics which were stamped with the designs on the skirt lengths like our border prints today. The Sears and Roebuck catalogue usually shows a few muslin prints which are small enough for this purpose. Another method for getting a design small enough for these little dolls is to use organdy as the fabric, trace the design very lightly in pencil and paint it with Prang Textile paints, available in most art and hobby shops. If you do not ever plan to wash the dress, of course, you may use water colors. I take most of the designs from the embroidery patterns in Godey's and Peterson's, which are certainly of the period, and easily adapted to color. They also are shown in varied sizes, so that you can usually find a design to fit your needs. There is a transfer pencil, sold by the Frederick Herrschner Company of Chicago, Illinois which will be of some help to you. Their catalog is worth sending for.

#18 - HOME DRESS   This dress should be made of a tiny print cotton. Trim the skirt as indicated on the diagram with ruffle of contrasting material. You may use silk ribbon, or you may make the ruffles of fabric. They should not be too full. The original dress had small bunches of wild flowers showing some foliage and was trimmed with a soft green. Do not mount the skirt on a waistband.

Join the side backs to the backs. Hem the backs. Sew shoulder seams. Trim the neckline with a ruffle. There should be a ruffle of narrow lace just barely visible above the heading of the ruffle. Gather the top of the sleeve to fit the **armscye**. Sew sleeve to **armscye**. Trim the bottom with two ruffles. Place a ruffle of half inch lace underneath the bottom ruffle of fabric so that it barely shows. Run a gathering thread along the bottom of the front of the bodice. Put the bodice on the doll and draw up the bottom of the bodice so that it fits the doll's waist. Sew the bodice and the skirt together. Make a belt to match the ruffles and fasten it in the front with either a small buckle or button.

You should make a small picture hat of straw for the doll to wear with this dress. To make these round hats draw a circle on a piece of cardboard. Cut a piece of straw long enough to go around the circle and sew the ends together. Dampen the straw and carefully pin around the circle. Let dry. Sew straw round and round until you have built up the inside of the circle. Dampen the hat again and push up a little mound in the center. Tie this over a thing (?) that is round and of the same size. When it is dry this time it is ready to trim. The hat which was originally made to go with this dress was of white straw. It had a black lace scarf across the back and a bunch of wild flowers (artificial) in the front. This dress can also be made in a white gauze of light silk, with contrasting ruffles of silk for evening wear. It can then be trimmed with garlands of small flowers.

#19 - AFTERNOON DRESS
Make the skirt of a pastel silk. The original was mauve. Trim, as in picture, with two bands of lace, which you have dyed to match skirt fabric. The bodice is made of a darker shade of the skirt material, lined with the skirt material.

Make the darts in the bodice front and backs. Join shoulder seams. Trim with two rows of very narrow black lace as shown in picture. Sew black jet beads down front to represent buttons. Sew right underarm seam. Line postillion. Trim to match bodice. Gather to fit between darts on back of bodice. Sew in place. Put lining in bodice, leaving left underarm open. Make bows of very narrow tubing of self-material, trimmed with black lace. Tack in place on shoulders and center back waist. Close underarm with tiny hooks and eyes. Wear over the blouse (pattern #41). Make one of the bonnets in harmonizing colors.

Bands of embroidery may be substituted for the lace on the skirt if you prefer. You may also make a canezou (pattern #42) to match, and a belt similar to the one given for wear with the traveling dress. That way, worn with the blouse you have an entirely different outfit.

Victorian ladies had almost as many ways of dressing their hair as (collectively) they had heads. They twisted it and knotted it; they curled it and they frizzed it. They draped it with flowers and swathed it with scarves. A ball room full of dancing debutants, seen from the air, might have resembled a waltzing flower garden. Those of you with dolls that have fixed hairdos, like the Chinas, will have to resort to little dots of glue (a water soluable one, if you please) most of these but you whose dolls have artificial locks can use your imigination to its fullest. False curls in tiny pins, chignons, wreathes and garlands, lace caps - all will be fun to make and charming on the doll. A few suggestions are given under the head wear section - which is where this should be of course, but there is not enough room. Just remember, the ladies almost always had something on their heads.

- 13 -

#20 - VISITING DRESS   This dress should be made of very lightweight silk in a pale lavender shade. Trim skirt according to the diagram with ruffles of lace one half inch wide. A ruching of darker lavender silk ribbon one fourth of an inch wide should be used as a heading for the ruffles. Do not set the skirt on to a waistband. Make darts in bodice front and backs. Hem back edges. Sew shoulder seams. Whip a very narrow lace ruffle around neckline. Set sleeves into armscye. Trim sleeve bottoms with two lace ruffles and a ruching of ribbon. Sew underarm seams. Close back with three tiny buttons, and buttonholes. Gather top of skirt to fit bodice and sew together. Sew a hook and eye to waist in the back. Make two small bows of the lavender ribbon. Sew one to the neckline and one to the waist at center front. Attach the one at the waistline by its outer loops only, to permit the ends of the fichu to pass through. Hem the inside curve of the fichu as far as the X. Trim the other edge, indicated by the solid line, with a double ruffle of narrow lace and a ruching of lavender ribbon. Make false sleeves (#40) and a bonnet in a harmonizing color to go with this dress.

Throughout this booklet I have given the colors for the garments. They are meant to be a guide so that you will know what color would have been appropriate for the period. You need not use these exact colors. The Victorians went more to extremes in their choice of colors than we do today. Pastels were very pale and colors were generally more vivid. Magenta, electric blue, a vivid kelly green, and scarlet were colors frequently mentioned (although not necessarily by those names). They were used in combinations with white or black, and paler shades of one another. Brown was popular. Unrelieved black was reserved for mourning dress exclusively. It has always seemed to me that small dolls look better in lighter colors - perhaps because the pale colors emphasize their daintiness more than brighter colors. Prints, small and floral, and checked ginghams are also appropriate to the period.

- 14 -

#21 - TRAVELING DRESS   Make according to petticoat (#7) measurements, a petticoat of black and white stripped taffeta (if the taffeta is unavailable, substitute poplin). Trim the bottom with two half inch ruffles of self-material. Pipe the lower edges in scarlet. Make skirt of tan poplin. Trim bottom with two rows of very narrow black velvet ribbon. To the bottom edge of each row of ribbon sew jet beads about one half inch apart. Mount the skirt on a narrow waistband. Make a skirt suspender (#11) to hold skirt up in front and reveal the striped petticoat. Make the belt of poplin. Line it with taffeta. Trim as in picture with ribbon and jet beads. Place a hook and eye at center back.

Make the jacket of poplin, lined with taffeta. Sew darts in front. Sew back side pieces to center back. Sew shoulder seams. Set sleeves in armscye. Sew underarm seams. Trim, as in picture, with black velvet and beads. Close with button and loop at center front. The doll should wear the outfit over the blouse (#41). Make the toque (#32) in harmonizing colors.

Traveling suits such as this one provided aid to both North and South during the Civil War. Beneath their voluminous skirts, the traveling ladies sometimes concealed little goodies to help the war effort on both sides. A partial inventory of the period shows what these ladies packed in trunks when they traveled; cambric petticoats; chemises; kerchiefs; hosiery; every day fan of colored parchment; lace fan; smelling salts; headache powder; ball room mantilla; boots; taffeta visiting dress; prayer book; pin cushion; sleeping bonnet; lap robe.

This combination of skirt, blouse, jacket, and cape was very popular in this period. Never before had women worn skirts and blouses. Much of the charm of the costumes of the period results from the delightful ways they applied this new concept of clothing. The many types of jackets which the ladies wore either over plain dresses or over blouses keep the pages of Godey's lively with variety. They should also lend variety to your doll's wardrobe.

- 15 -

#22 - DINNER DRESS   Make this dress of a delicate yellow silk. Trim the skirt according to the diagram with a ruching of a deeper shade of yellow silk ribbon. If you prefer you may substitute narrow velvet ribbon. If you use velvet ribbon, don't try to ruch it. Sew a slightly gathered ruffle of one half inch lace around the edges of the ruching, and just underneath. The gathering of the lace should be concealed by the ribbon. Gather top of the skirt and mount on a narrow waistband. Close the back with a hook and eye.

Sew darts in front and backs. Hem backs. Sew shoulder seams. Bind neck edge with narrow self-binding. Trim with a row of lace sewed flat. Add an extra row of lace just in the front. Sew sleeve to **armscye**. Face the bottom of the sleeves back with self-material. Trim the top of the base of the sleeve with ruching and lace similar to the skirt, but use lace only one fourth of an inch wide. Gather top of sleeve to fit **armscye**. Bind bottom of bodice narrowly with self-material.

Face back the inside curve of the fichu. Trim the bottom with a double ruffle of one fourth inch lace separated by a ruching of the ribbon. Close the back of the bodice with three small buttons and a hook and eye at the waist, sew a small eye under each arm, and the corresponding hook at the points of the fichu. A bow with long streamers may be tied around the waist, in the front. The dress should be worn over the false sleeves. This is another one of those dresses which may be easily varied and adapted to different uses. It may be made in a variety of fabrics. For instance, you could use a tiny gingham check, making the fichu of organdy.

The skirt trim may be shortened, and reversed, so that it runs up the skirt, rather than down. In that case it should extend about one third of the way up the skirt. Or you may use a ruffle of self-material, edged with lace, and headed with a ruching of the ribbon. Take care that the ruffles are not too full or the skirt will balloon out in an ungraceful manner.

#23 - EVENING DRESS   The skirt of the underdress should be made of fine white tulle or chiffon. It should be trimmed for a distance of about one third of the way up with a shirring of self-material. Cut the shirring piece twice the width of your skirt and about one inch deeper than the depth you wish to cover. Put the shirring threads in, pin to skirt, and adjust gathers. Tack in place. Sew the skirt to a waistband.

The front and back of the bodice should be lined with white silk. Make darts in front and backs. Hem back edges. Gather tops of sleeves to fit the armscye. Sew sleeves to armscye. Turn bottom of sleeve under. Whip a piece of one fourth inch lace to the edge. Gather bottom of sleeve to fit arm. Sew underarm seam. Trim neckline and bottom of bodice with ruffles of narrow lace. Close backs with small snaps. Sew little pearls down front to simulate buttons.

The coatee should be made of blue silk lined with white, and trimmed with black lace. Sew back side pieces to back. Make darts in fronts. Sew shoulder seams. Trim **armscye** with ruffle of narrow lace. Sew underarm seams. Trim all edges except lower bottom of back with ruffles of narrow lace. Be sure that the ruffles are sewn to the very edge. Sew a one and a half inch lace ruffle to the back. Sew a little pearl to x on left front, and a loop to right front. Fold the revers over and press. You may add garlands of small artificial flowers down the back of the over dress and around the neckline of the under dress in the front, if you wish. If you do, you should also scatter them on the shirred band. The under dress may be used alone as a dress with the addition of a sash, or a fichu or bertha. Made in a small gingham check with a harmonizing sash it will make a nice summer dress for a young girl - such as Scarlet to wear to the picnic. The shirring should be omitted if the dress is to be made for daytime wear. Ruffles of self material or lace, or eyelet may be substituted. A wide circular straw hat may be made for the summer dress.

#24 - BALLGOWN This dress is made of pale blue tulle. Cut two net skirts by your skirt pattern. Cover one entirely with one half inch ruffles of self-material, slightly gathered. Cut a third skirt of net slightly larger than the others. Put hems in all three skirts. Place them togehter - plain skirt on the bottom, then the ruffled one, and finally the large skirt. Gather them to fit waist and mount on a waistband.

For the bodice back and front use (#23) evening dress under dress pattern. Make the bodice of tulle lined with silk. Sew darts. Hem backs. Sew shoulder seams. Make the sleeves of net. Sew narrow net ruchings to lines across center of sleeves. Gather tops of epaulettes and baste to top of sleeve. Gather top of sleeve to fit **armscye**. Sew in place. Gather bottom of sleeve to fit arm. Narrowly bind with pale blue satin. Bind neck and bottom of bodice in a similar manner. Make the front folds of one layer of tulle. Gather on dotted lines as tightly as possible. Sew in place to shoulder and underarm seams as shown in picture. Close back with three small buttons and a hook at waistline. The entire dress should be sprinkled with little silver beads sewn in place. Bows of narrow blue satin should be placed at each shoulder. The skirt decoration is made of two pieces of one inch ribbon caught twice by bows of narrow ribbon. These decorations may be placed all around the skirt at regular intervals, if you wish. When Elisabeth, Empress of Austria was married she had a most marvelous trousseau. I include the list here to give you an idea of what the Victorians considered necessary: 14 high-necked dresses, 6 dressing gowns; 19 summer frocks (she was married in May); 4 ball room crinolines; 16 bonnets; 6 coats; 8 mantillas; 5 mantelets; 14 dozen chemises; 14 dozen pairs stockings; 6 dozen petticoats; 5 dozen pantelets; 1 dozen boudoir wraps; 6 pairs of boots; 6 pairs of slippers; and 20 pairs of gloves; and 20 dozen handkerchiefs.

#25 - WEDDING DRESS   Make the underskirt of satin and the overskirt of fine tulle or lace. Cut both by skirt pattern, adding a little in the back for the train. Trim the bottom of the overskirt with three rows of one inch lace, slightly gathered. Make skirt panels of white satin lined with tulle. The embroidery is done with white silk floss. You will probably have to use rayon floss. Place the panels at equal distances around the ungathered skirt. Baste to top of skirt. You may use four or six panels, as you choose. Gather over and underskirt together and mount on waistband.

Make the bodice of satin. Cut back of bodice and sleeve by Evening Dress underdress (#17) pattern. Place tucked tulle over area indicated on wedding dress bodice pattern. Baste in place. Sew darts in front. Work embroidery as indicated over edge of tulle. Sew shoulder seams. Make the sleeves of satin. Gather to fit armscye. Sew to **armscye**. Gather bottom of sleeve to fit arm. Bind the bottom of the sleeves. Sew underarm seam. Hem backs. Close with tiny buttons and buttonholes. Narrowly bind neckline and bodice bottom of bodice.

The embroidery is to be worked in outline, satin stitch, and French knots. If you prefer you may substitute garlands of tiny artificial flowers. This dress is meant to be worn at a very formal wedding, hence the low neck and short sleeves. Actually any of the dresses, except the travelling suit, can be used as a wedding dress pattern. Satin, velvet, and lace were the materials most commonly used for wedding dresses in the 1860's, even as they are now. Your doll's accessories should include a blue garter, a one inch square handkerchief monogrammed and trimmed with lace, and a bouquet of tiny white flowers. You might also want to make her a little prayer book of white satin. Mitts may be made of white lace, double edged. Cut the lace wide enough to fit around doll's hand and whip raw edges together. Catch the edge of the lace together between the thumb and palm. Mitts are a suitable accessory for any dress of the period.

HEAD WEAR

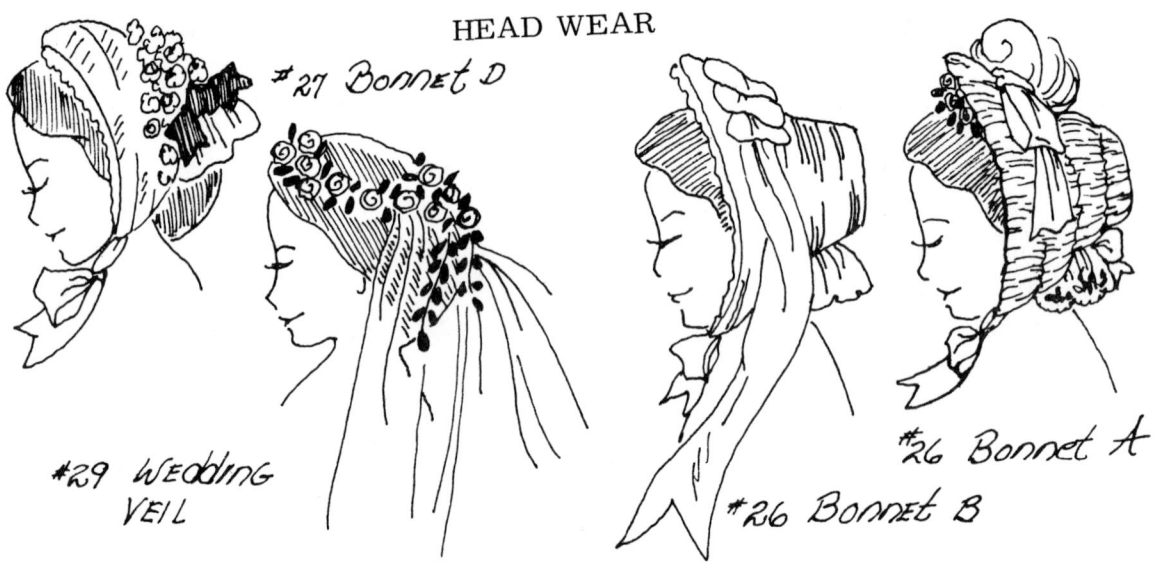

#29 Wedding Veil
#27 Bonnet D
#26 Bonnet B
#26 Bonnet A

#26 - LARGE BONNET Make the base or form, of buckram. Lay one end of the crown over the other and glue together. Make small slashes as indicated in pattern. Fold in on dotted line. Glue the top of the crown in place. Slash the inside curve of brim and glue it in place around the brim. This larger bonnet was the most popular form in the early part of the period. It may be covered in silk or velvet or made of straw. To make the form of straw trace the patterns onto cardboard. Omit the seam allowance. Proceed according to instructions given for the picture hat (page 12) and whip the finished pieces together.

BONNET A Cover large bonnet form with white silk, shirred to fit on the outside. The inside should be smoothly covered. Place a ruffle of one fourth inch lace and a spray of small flowers just underneath the inside of the brim. Sew a one half inch lace ruffle across the back of the brim, forming the "curtain". A small bow should be placed at center back over the curtain. A larger flat bow should be placed over the top of the brim with a few ostrich plumes as a plume. Two narrow ribbons are stitched to the inside of the brim at X's for ties.

BONNET B Make large bonnet form of white straw. (One yard of one fourth inch straw is sufficient to make these bonnets.) Whip a length of scarlet ribbon, shirred, to the inside of the brim. Whip a ruffle of one fourth inch lace to the back edge of the ribbon. Box pleat a piece of ribbon to go over the top of the brim. Leave streamers long enough to reach half way down doll's chest. Catch pleats with jet beads. Box pleat another length of ribbon for the curtain. Trim with beads. Make chin ties of narrow black ribbon. If you wish you may sew a ruffle of black lace so that it just shows underneath the curtain.

#27 - SMALL BONNET This bonnet is also made of either buckram or straw. There is no sewing. Make the straw according to previous instructions. Sew the curtains between notches in back. Chin ties are sewn to X's.

BONNET C Cover the small form with white silk. Cover the outside with ruffles of quarter inch white lace. Dot jet beads here and there over the lace. Sew a bow of white ribbon and some small pink flowers at center back. Chin ties of white are sewn to X's. A ruching of white tulle and some more flowers form the inside brim trimming.

BONNET D Make small form of yellow straw. A lace ruffle and some small yellow and white flowers trims the inside of the brim. The curtain is of white lace trimmed with some ivy, or other foliage. Leaving about one half inch of the front of the brim plain cover the entire rest of the bonnet with small yellow and white flowers. Chin ties are of white ribbon.

#28 - SNOOD Use a pastel BARBIE doll net in a pastel shade. Cover the front half with a piece or quarter inch ribbon in a matching color ending with a loop and short streamer over each ear.

#29 - WEDDING VEIL Make a wreath of small flowers and gather to it a piece of lace or tulle measuring about thirteen by twenty-five inches. Run the gathering thread along the edge. The veil should be sewed to the back underneath the hanging flowers.

#30 - EVENING HEAD DRESS A Make five rosettes of very narrow silk ribbon. Gather as tightly as possible. Sew to a very narrow length of net, folded several times. Make loops and streamers of wider ribbon to cover net in back. Clusters of small flowers may be used instead of the rosettes.

#31 - EVENING HEAD DRESS B Make a flat bow with long streamers. Trim, according to picture with ruffles of one quarter inch ribbon.

#32 - TOQUE These little pill boxes were used for traveling or "sports" wear - for instance, croquet. They can be made of velvet or straw, or to match the dress. They were usually trimmed with feathers or fur. Make the form of buckram. Glue the two ends of the crown together. Whip the top on place. Cut a circle of fabric large enough to cover the brim. Gather the outside edge and draw up over the form. Fold the raw edges under the form and sew or glue in place. Trim as shown with a feather.

WRAPS

#33 - CAPUCHON Make this little capelet of a lightweight white wool. Line it with cherry colored satin. Sew seam AB. Trim hood with narrow black velvet ribbon or braid on solid line. Make a tassel of the finest white baby yarn. Sew to point of hood. Gather bottom of hood to fit neck of cape. Trim cape to match hood with velvet ribbon or braid. Sew cape and hood together. Trim all around with ruffle of narrow black lace or a ruching of black net. Sew narrow cherry colored ties to X's on cape.

#34 - SUMMER MANTLE Make this of white organdy. Cut a square of material measuring five inches square. Fold in half and press. Hem one triangle and trim with black velvet or braid. Make a ruffle of the organdy about two inches deep. Hem both ends and the bottom. Trim with black. Gather this to fit the edge of the other triangle. Fold the other part of the square over the ruffled part. Take care when you sew the trim on that it will be on the right side when you fold the top over.

#33 Capuchon

fold this part on top of lower triangle

#34 Summer mantle

#35 Burnouse

#36 Mantelet

#35 - BURNOUSE   This was one of the most popular forms of **wraps** in the period. Following the diagram make the pattern in the same manner the skirt pattern was made. Make the burnouse of white lace edged with a narrow edging. Sew white middy braid over the top edge of the lace. Tack together at X's. Sew rosettes made of middy braid to dots. Make ties and tassels of white crochet thread. Chain stitch the ties. Put another tassel at center back of the top. Ladies wore these capes as shawls, not tieing the strings and catching the front ends up over the arms. You may make it in black lace, as well as white. For winter wear it can be made in a lightweight wool or velvet and lined in a contrasting color.

#36 - MANTELET   The mantelet should be made of a light silk. As it is intended for evening wear it may be made in a color to match the dress with which it is to be worn. The silk should be lightly padded and quilted. Line it with white silk. Sew the shoulder seams. Narrowly bind all around with self-material. Close the front with three tiny bottons and loops. Trim the bottom with a ruffle of one and a half inch lace, or a ruffle of self-material edged with narrow lace.

ACCESSORIES

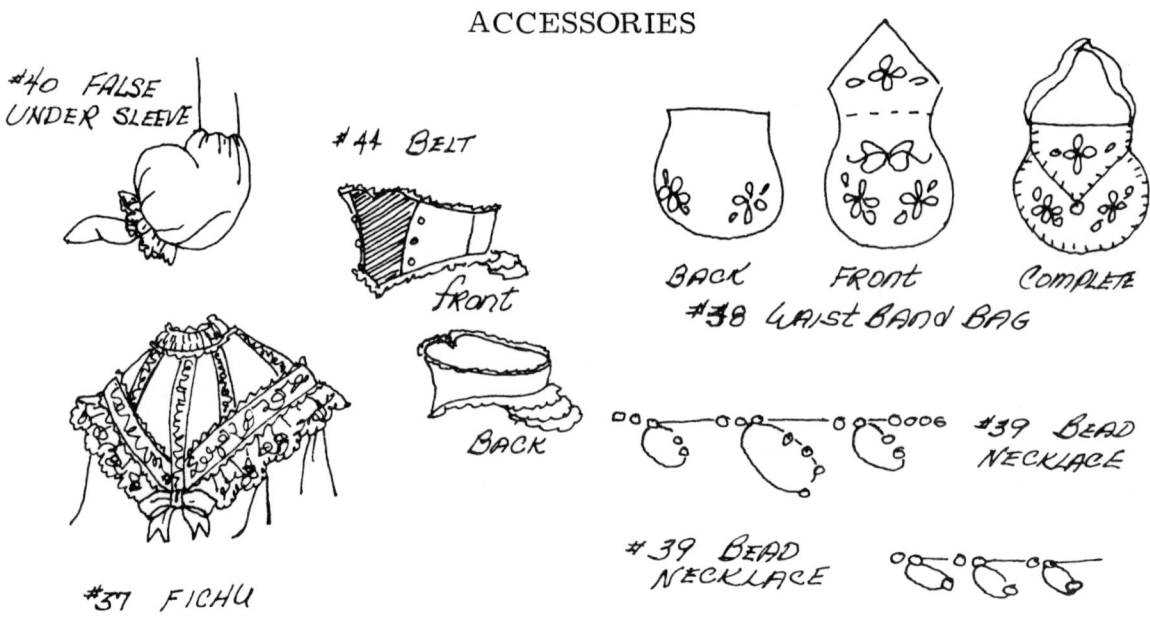

#37 - FICHU   This may be worn over any plain bodice, high or low-necked. Make it of tulle. Trim on shaded areas with a shirring of net. Trim on solid lines with very narrow insertion. Edge with a ruffle of narrow lace. Fold back edges under and hem. Close back with three small buttons and loops. Trim center front with a triple looped bow of quarter inch ribbon.

#38 - WAIST BAND BAG   Make this of silk to harmonize with the dress with which it is to be worn. Do the embroidery with single strand floss before you cut the pattern out. Lay front and back together. Buttonhole stitch together. Buttonhole stitch around opening. Close with a small button and loop. Sew loop of ribbon to either side and hang over belt or sash.

#39 - BEAD JEWELRY   String one bead on thread. Knot thread through it and sew to a small hook. String sixteen beads on thread. Loop thread through third bead back. String seven more beads. Loop thread through fifth bead back. String four more beads. Loop thread through third bead back. String fourteen more beads and sew small eye to last bead. You can vary this design by the number of beads you string before you loop the thread. Very often you can find suitable bits of beading on old garments. If carefully cut apart you can obtain pins, earrings, necklaces in this manner. You can also cut the designs out of discarded toothpaste tubes. Press (with an orange stick) little designs into the metal. Cement small stones in. Paint the metal gold.

#40 - FALSE UNDERSLEEVES   Cut two pieces of batiste two inches by five inches. Gather one long edge to fit over doll's hand. Narrowly bind it with self-material. Hem the other edge. Run elastic thread through the hem. Draw up to fit doll's arm. Seam short edges together.

#41 - BLOUSE Make the blouse of white lawn or batiste. Make pintucks in a piece of fabric large enough to cut the front and backs from. Cut pattern after pintucking is completed. Sew shoulder seams. Make pintucks in sleeve. Gather top of sleeves to fit. Sew sleeve to armscye. Gather bottom of sleeve to fit over hand. Sew underarm seam. Narrowly bind bottom of sleeve. Whip a ruffle of lace to binding. Sew a narrow binding down right front. Close front with button and buttonholes. Attach a lace collar to neckline. Hem bottom.

#42 - CANEZOU Make this of black lace. Sew shoulder and underarm seams. The shoulder should be left open below X's. Trim all edges with narrow bias banding of black satin. Put banding on line around armhole. Be sure to put the band on the right side of the revers after they are folded back. Trim all edges with one quarter inch lace slightly gathered. This should be worn over a plain silk dress made from pattern #17, the Robe Dress, omitting the trim shown and substituting instead plain bands of braid or ribbon on skirt. This may also be made up in silk or wool, with a skirt to match, and worn with a blouse. You may omit the little capes on the armscyes and set in loose sleeves, to make a winter jacket.

#43 - BOUQUET HOLDER Use a bell cap (used in jewelry work) a short piece of a flat toothpick, a short piece of chain and a jump ring (more jewelry). Fasten the ring to the chain, the chain through a hole in the toothpick. Glue toothpick to bell cap.

#44 - BELT Make the belt of black silk. Apply velvet to shaded areas. Trim all around with narrow black lace. Sew three lace ruffles to back. Close on left side. Trim with jet beads.

#45 - CRAVAT Cut two pieces of narrow velvet or silk ribbon long enough to go around doll's neck. Sew them together. Sew seed jet beads up center. Trim the ends with a narrow black lace ruffle. Close with a snap.

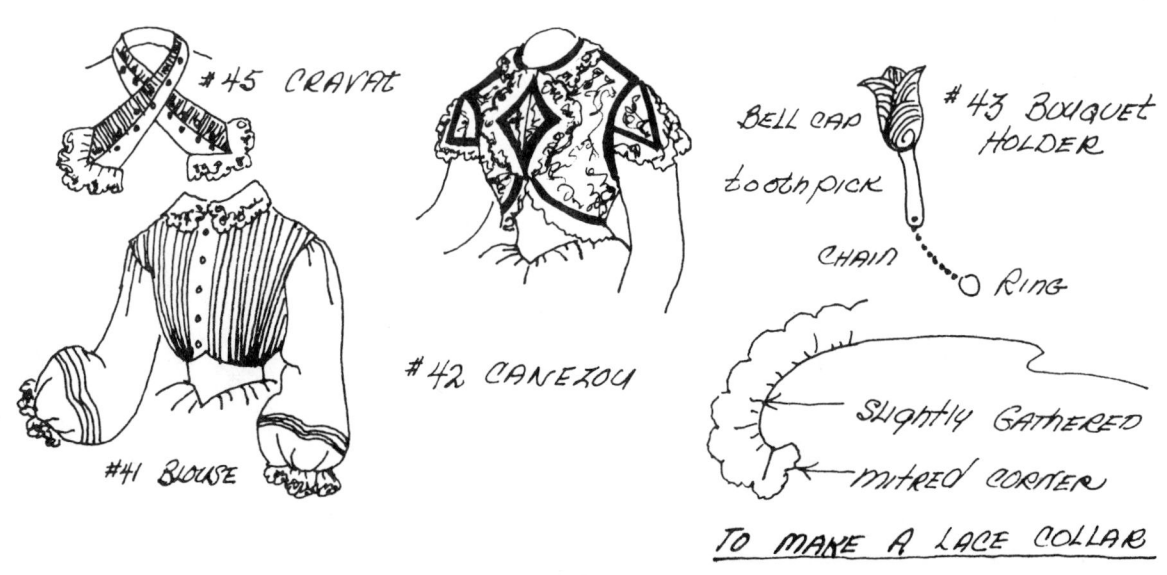

THE PATTERNS

With the exception of just a few patterns already given, all of the patterns are on the following pages. When you are ready to make one of the garments, I suggest that you trace it out of the book onto light-weight muslin, making note of all darts, notches, and other pertinent information. Then you may go right ahead and baste the pattern together to be sure that it fits just as you want it to. Then you can rip it apart and cut your fabric by the muslin. When you are through you can place the pattern pieces into an envelope where they will be safe until the next time you need them. Please be sure when you are tracing the patterns that you get all the pieces to the garment you are working on.

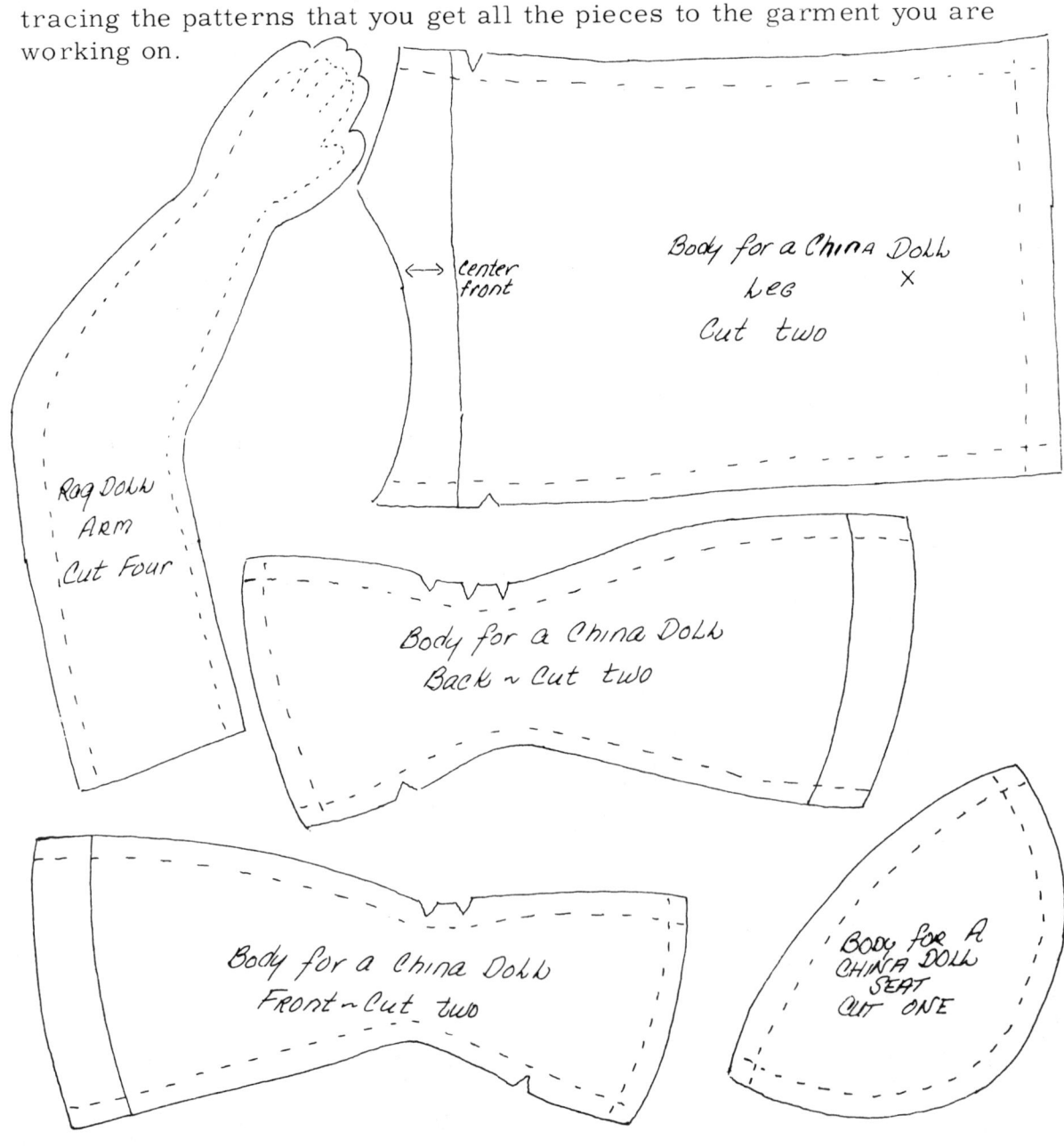

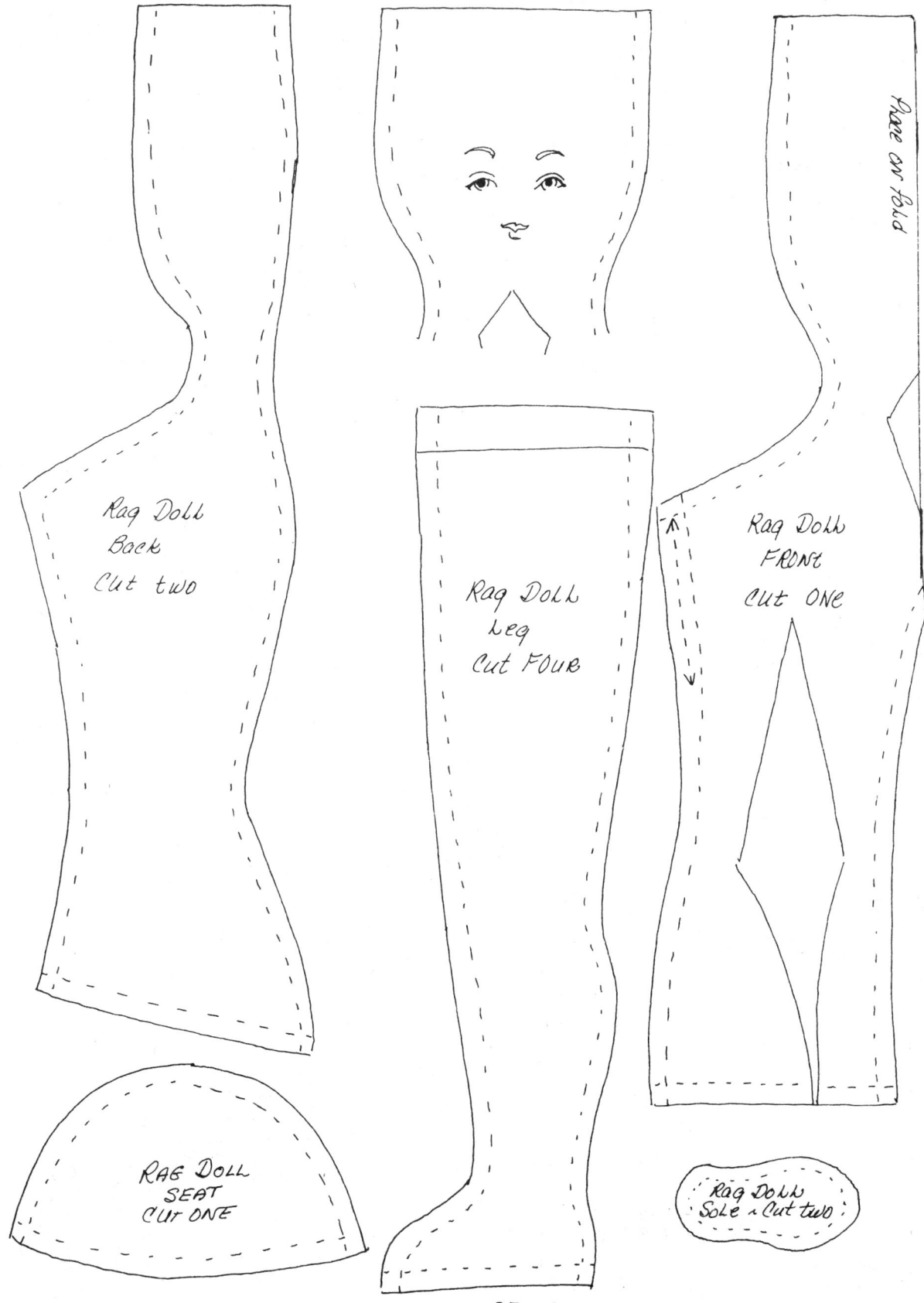

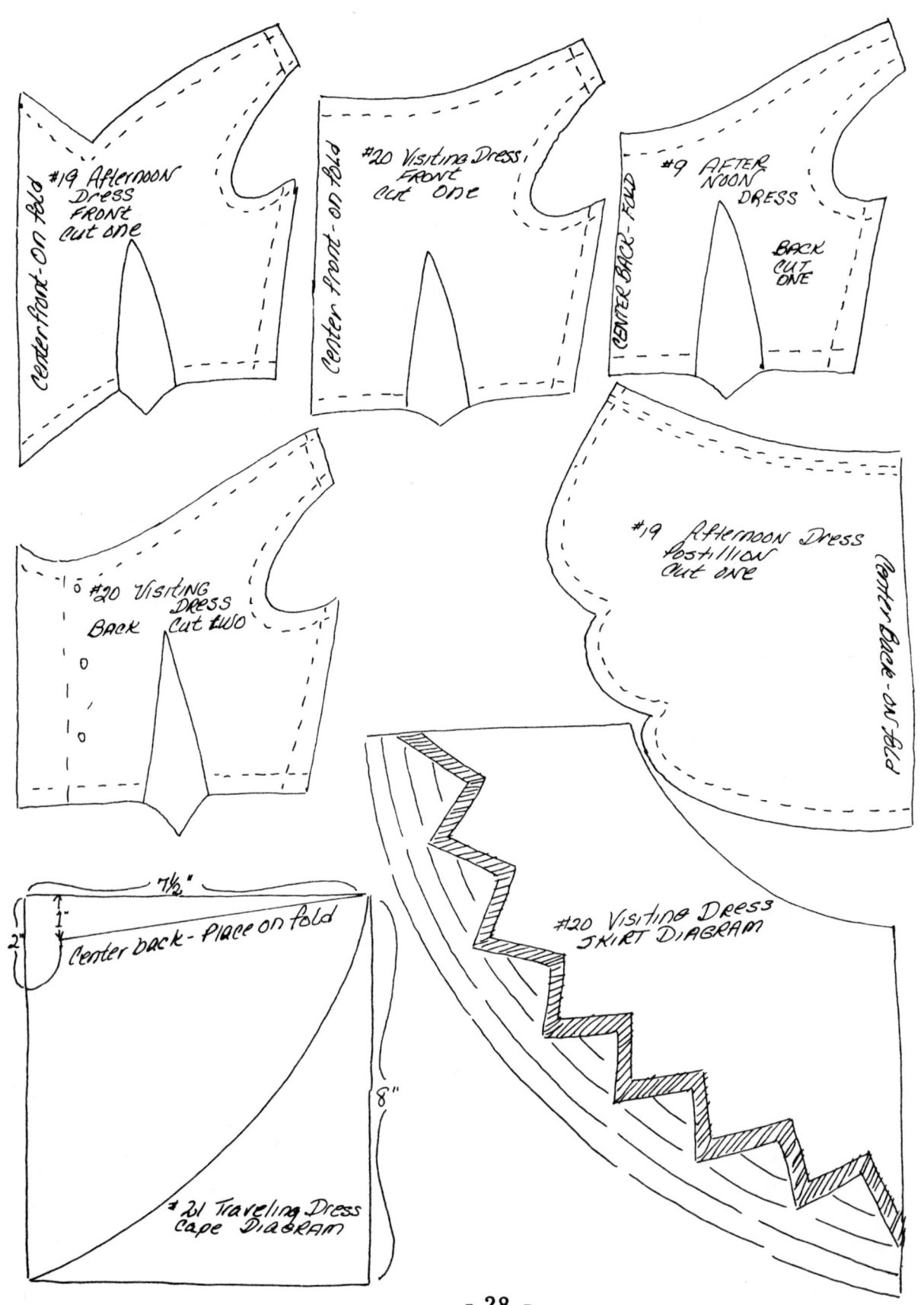

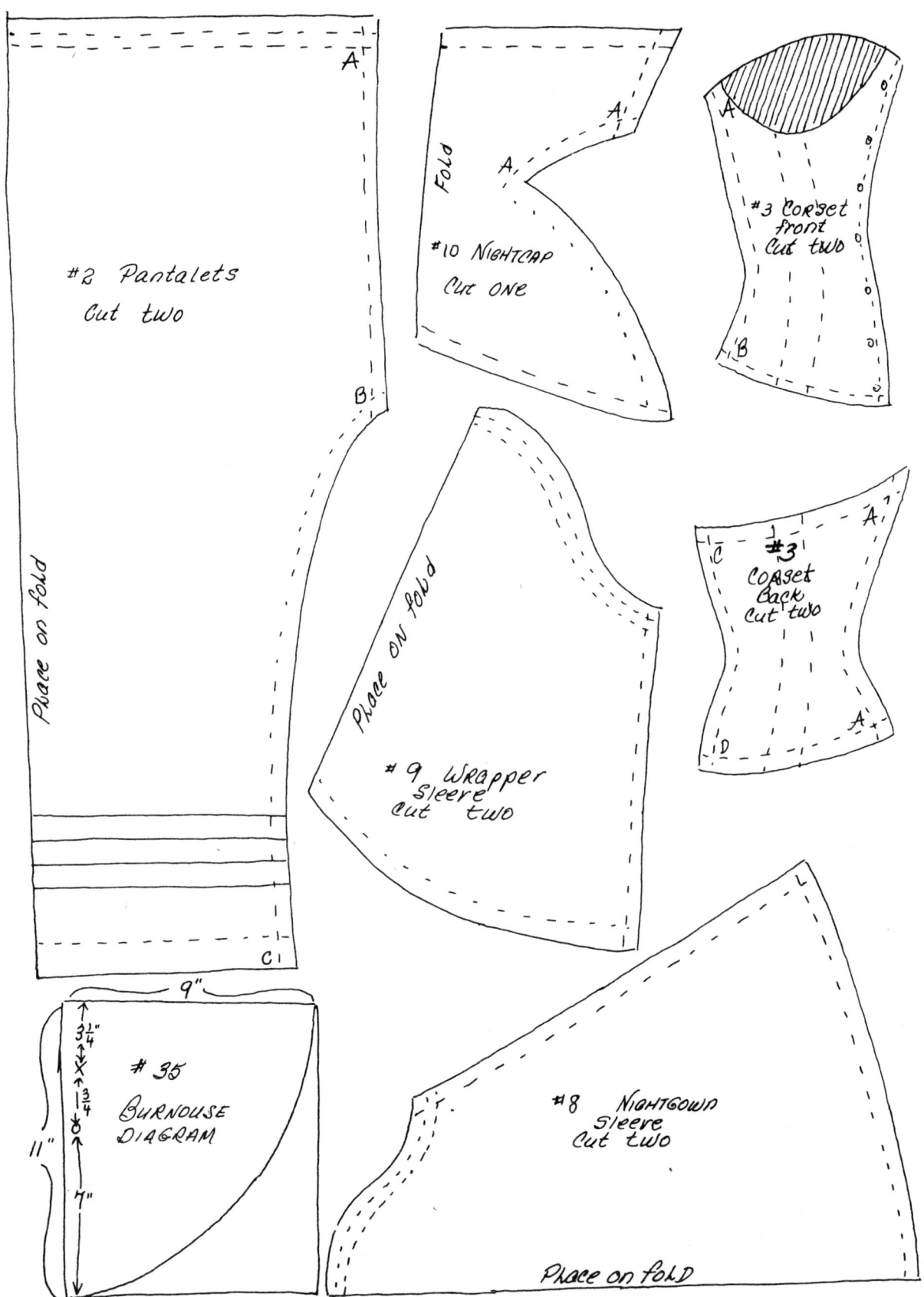

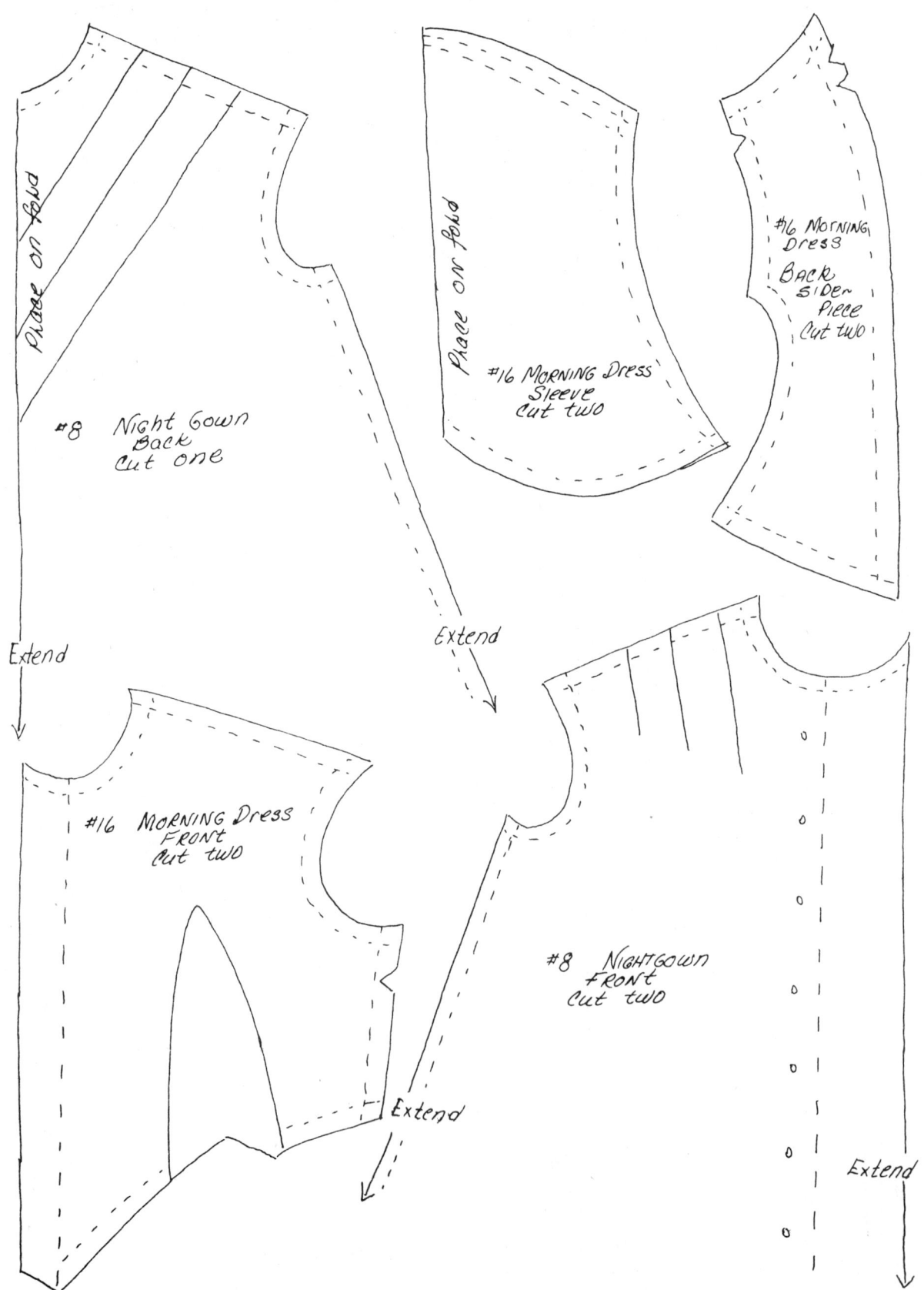

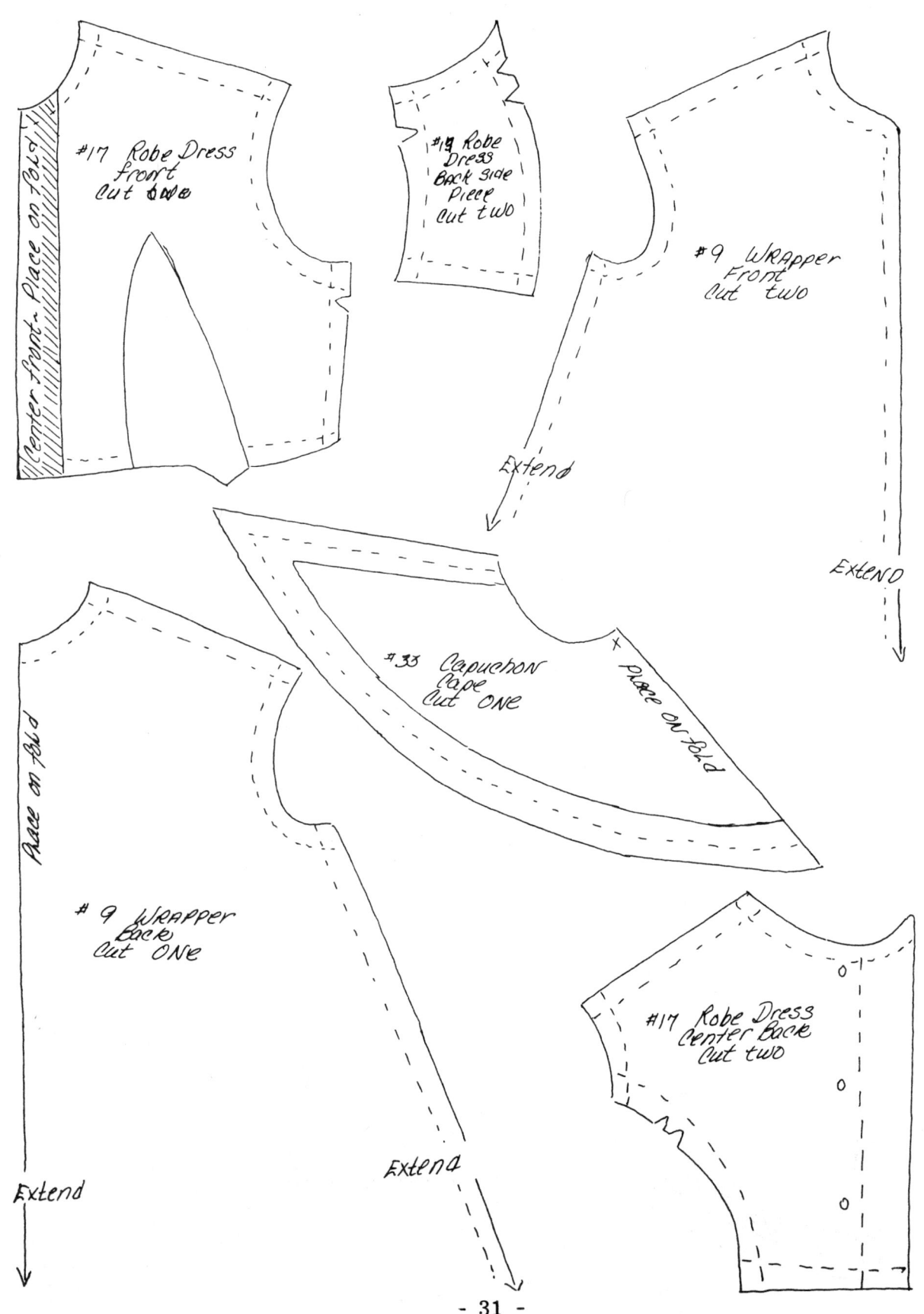

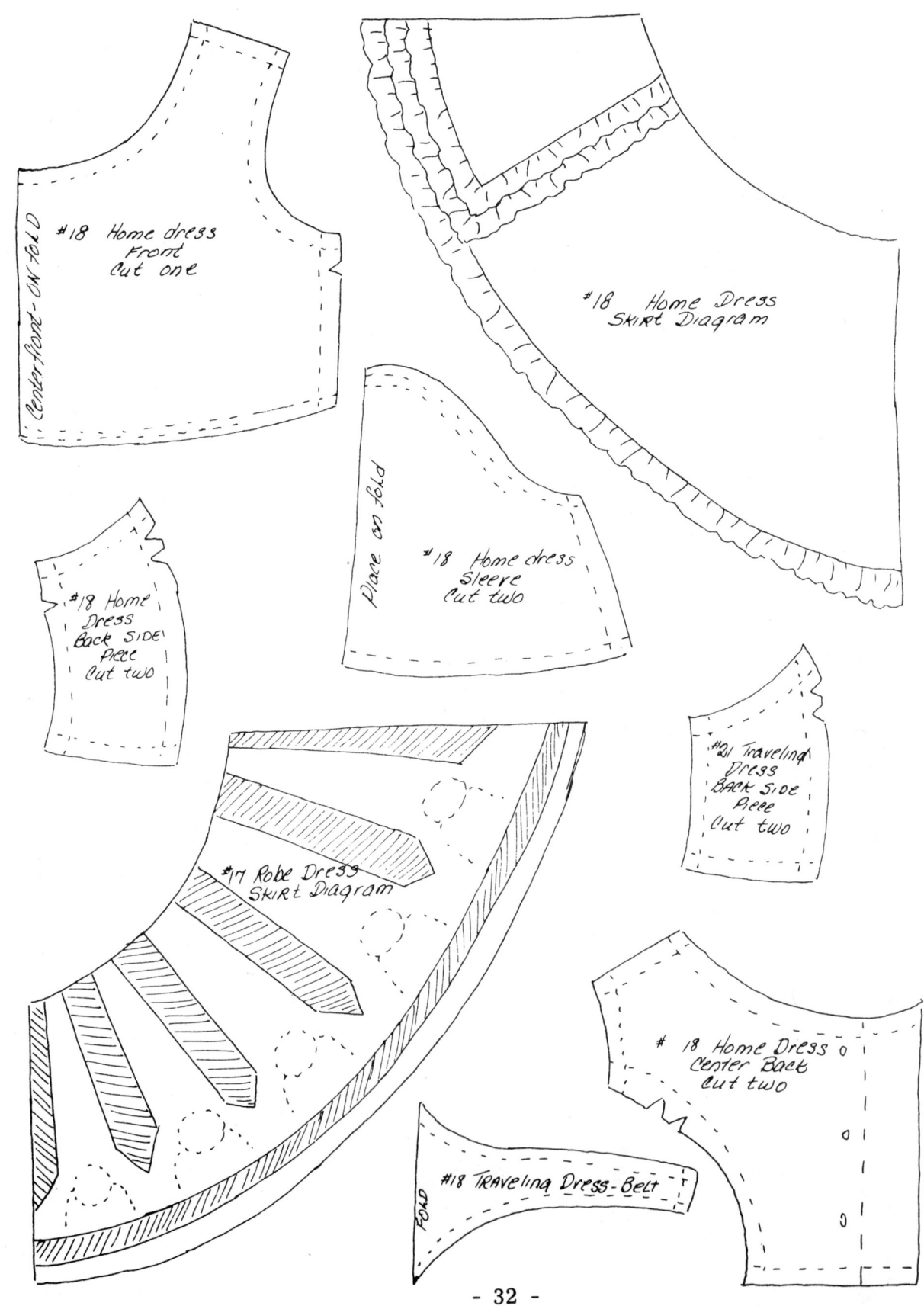

- 32 -

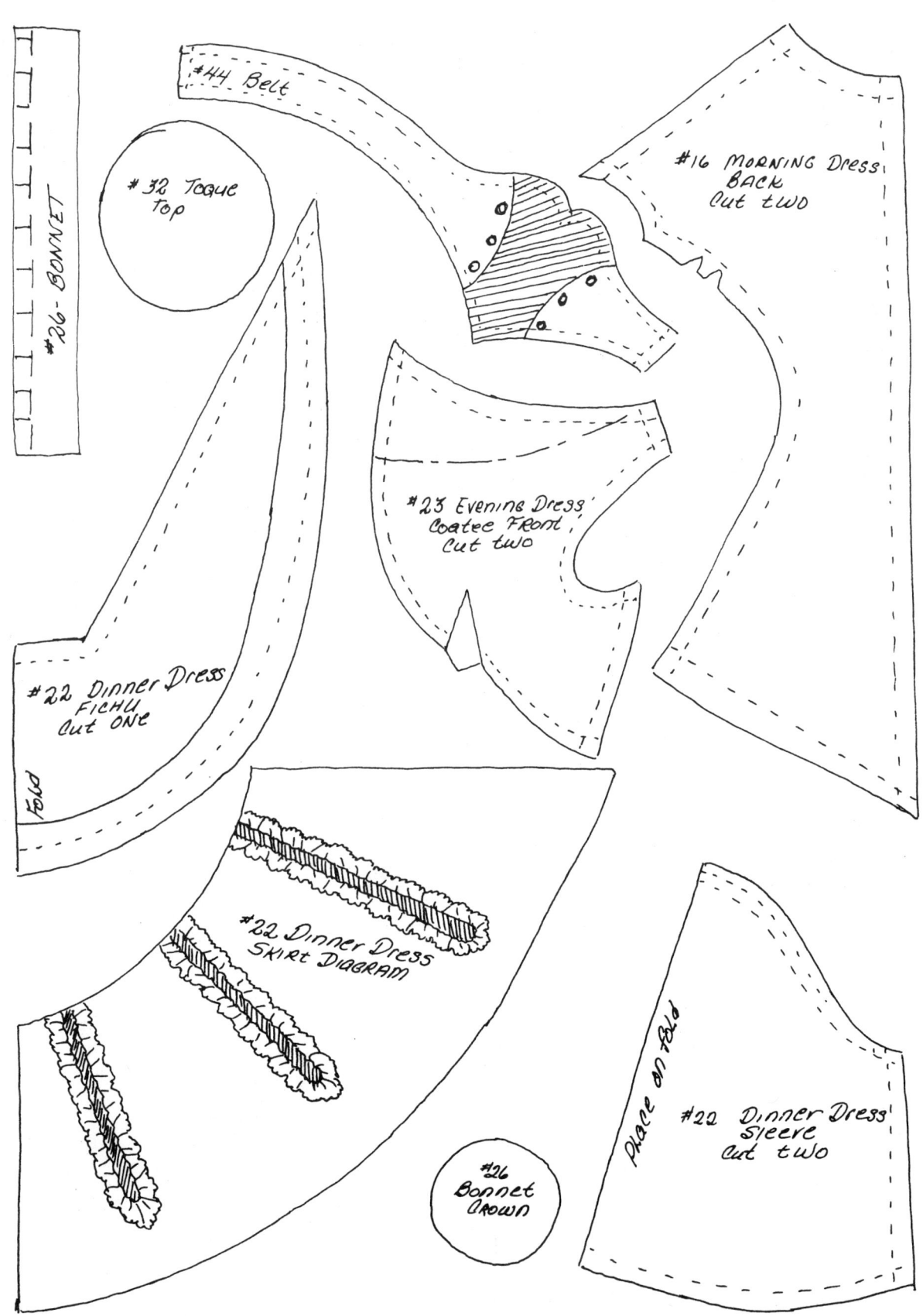

- 33 -

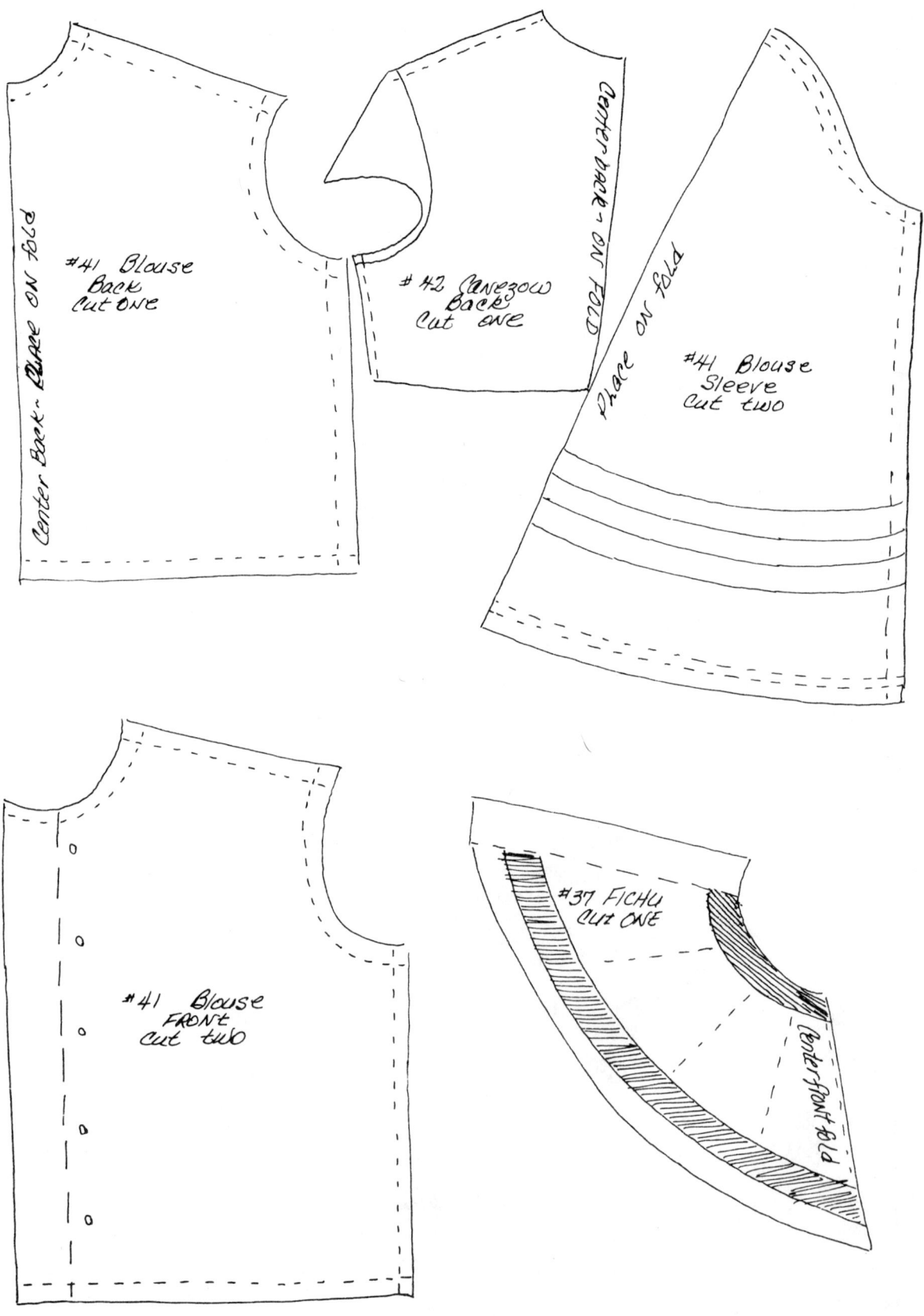

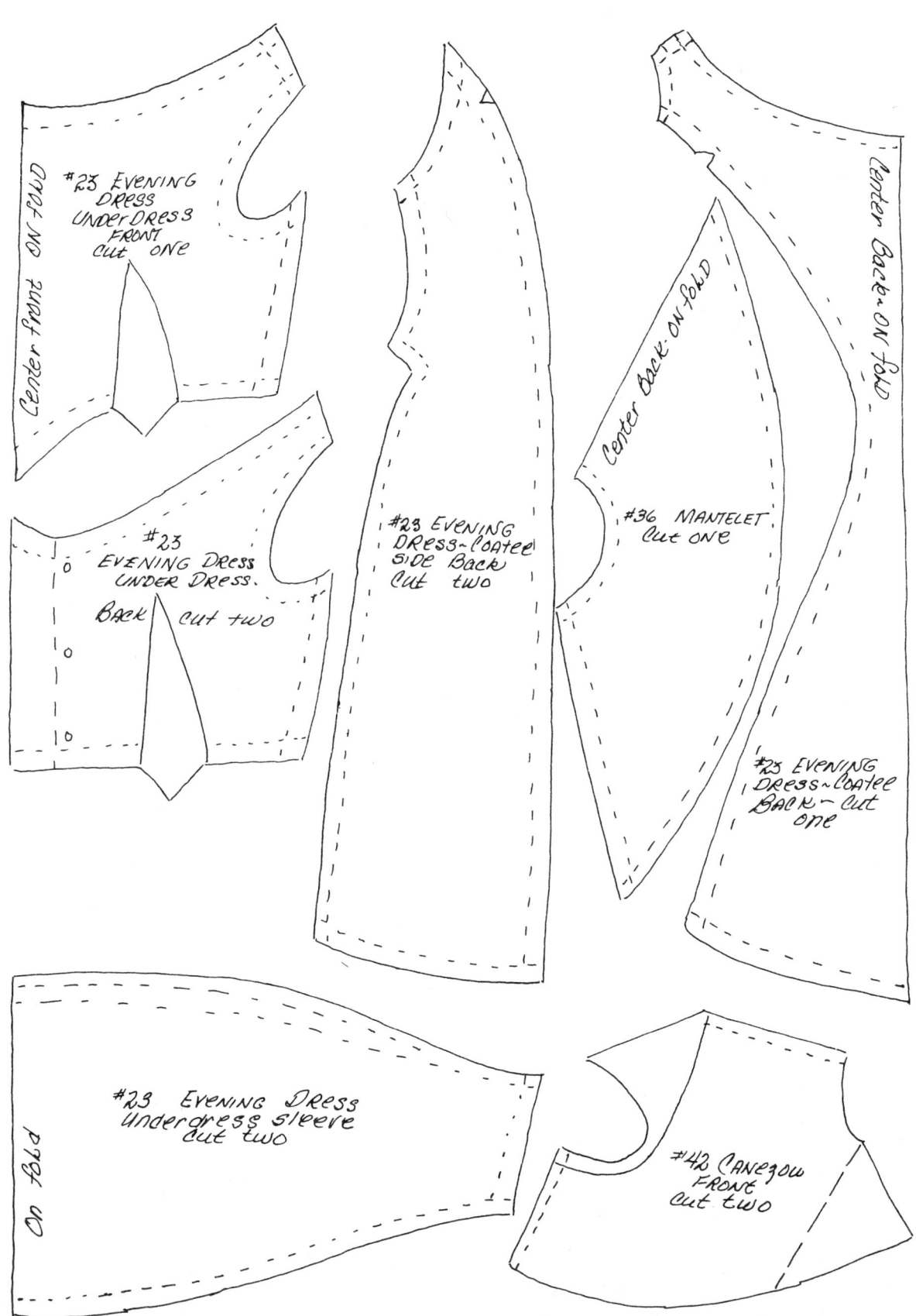

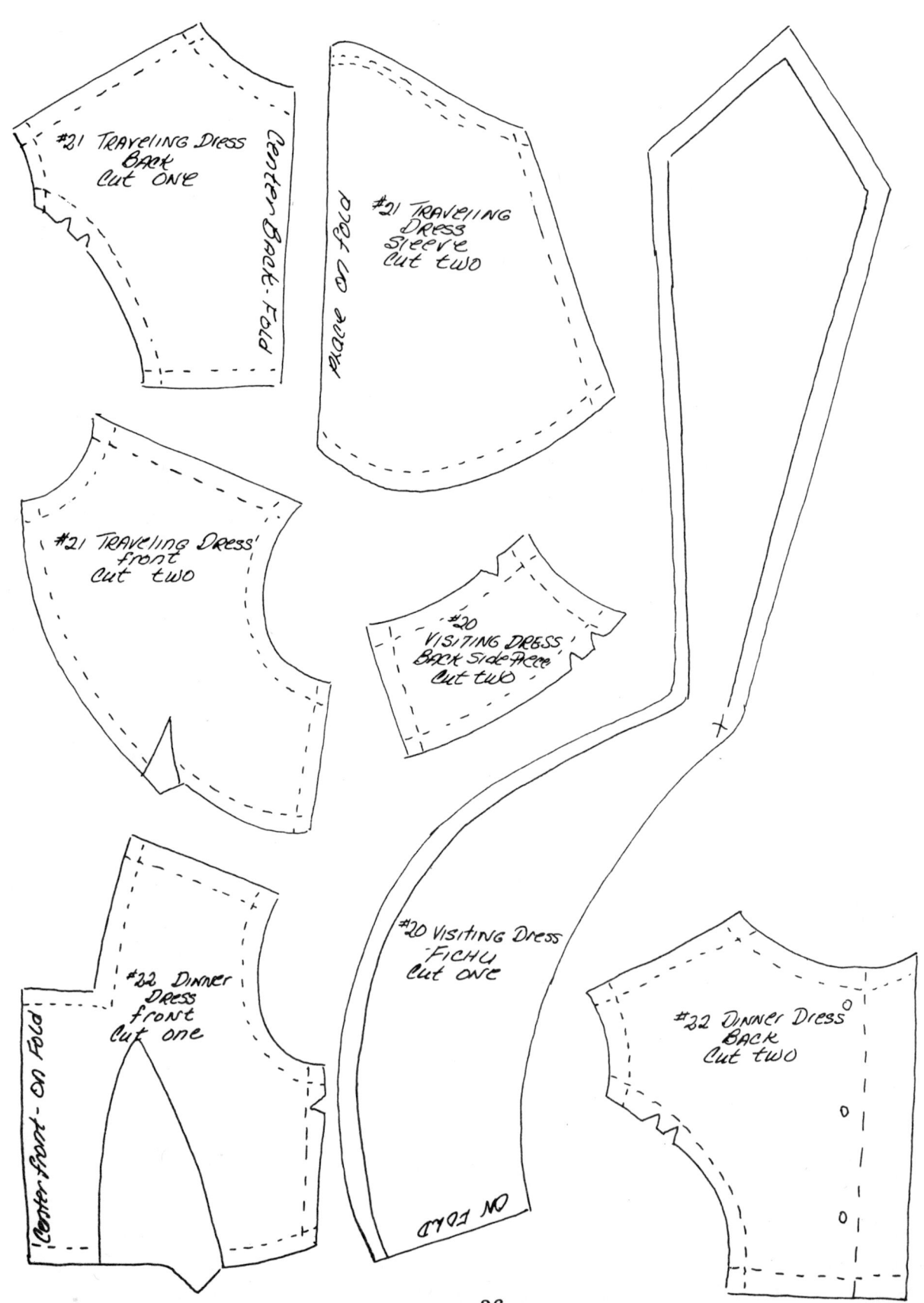

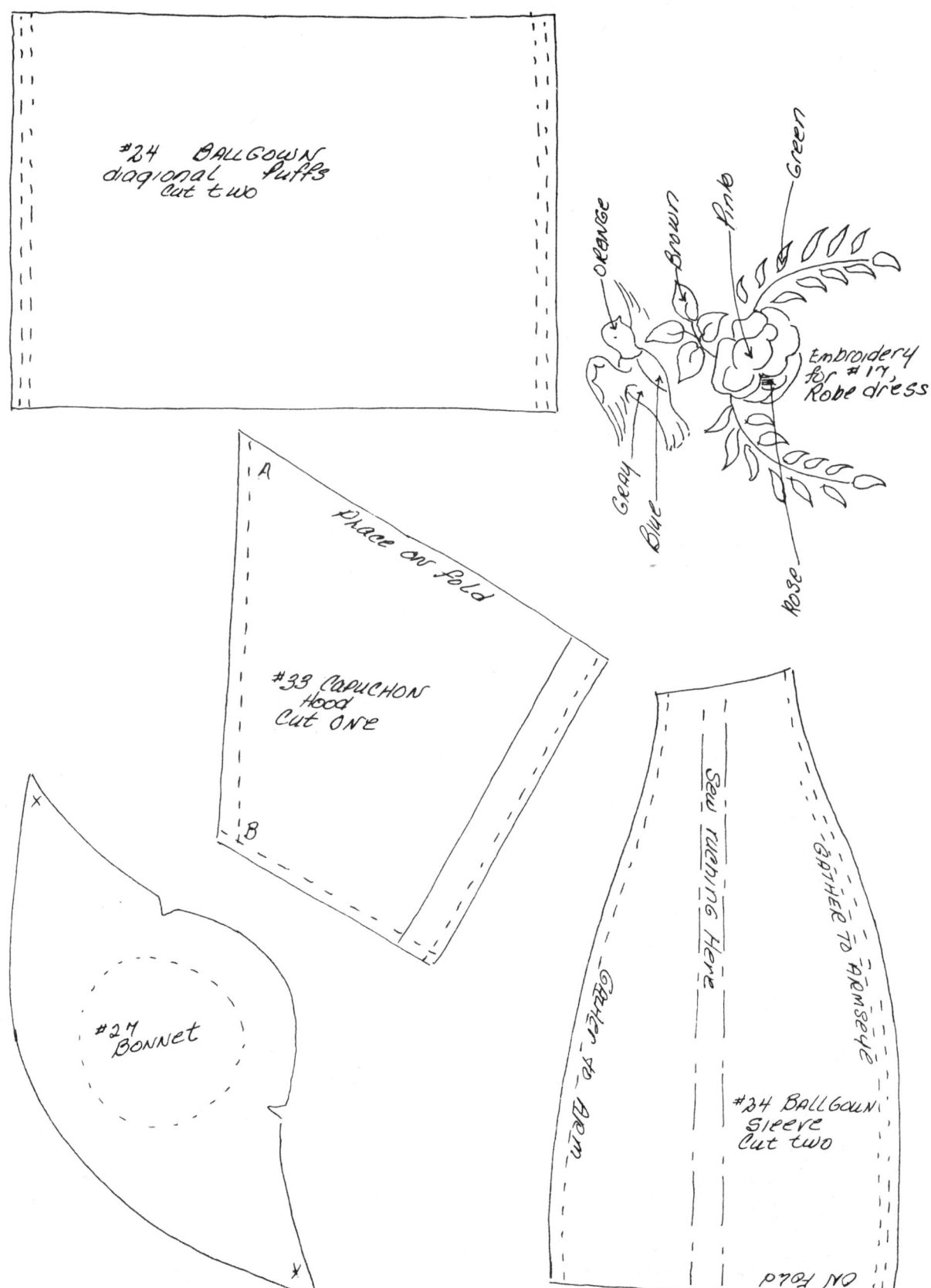

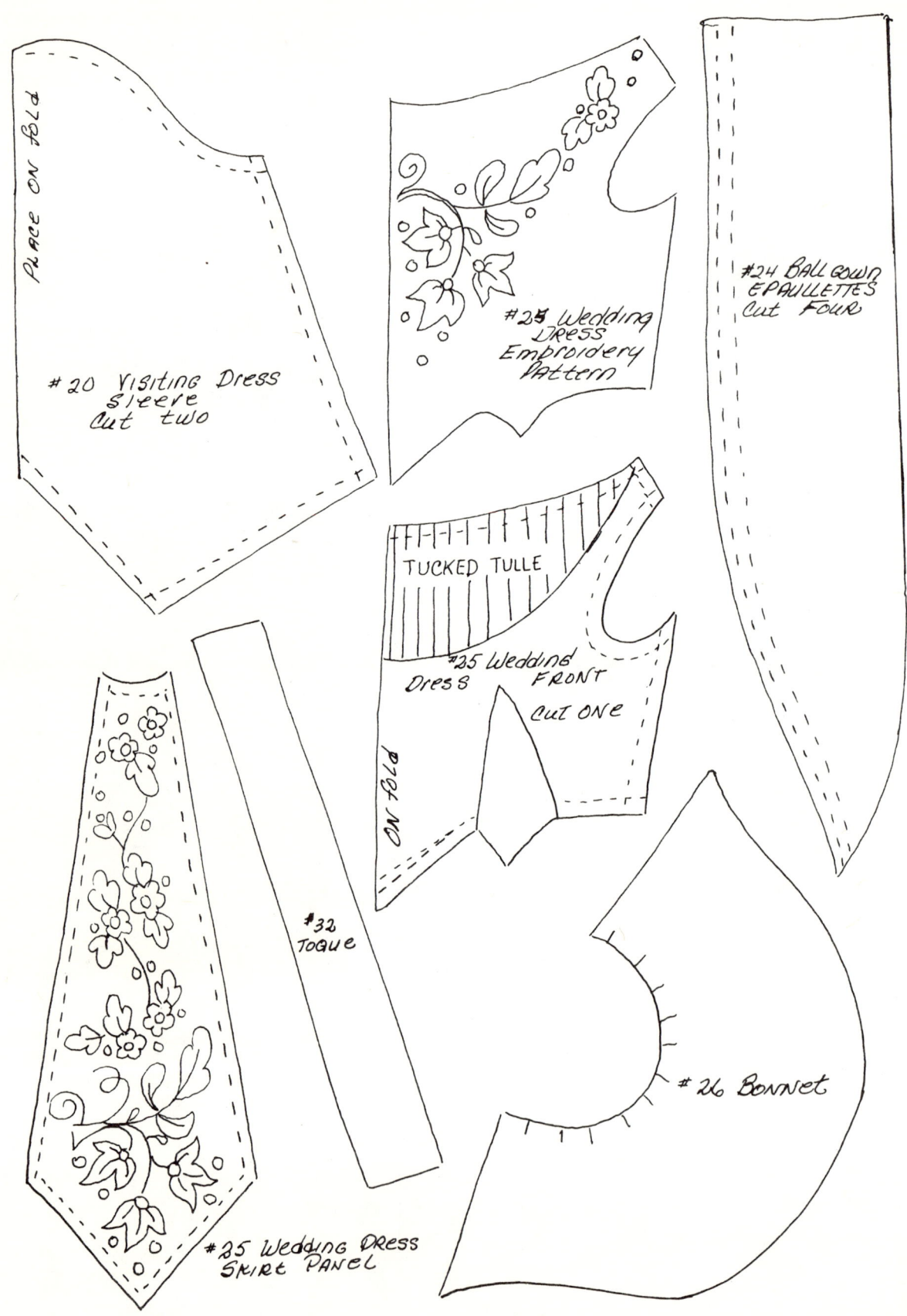